GOD LIKES ME
By Jen Priester

Copyright © 2018 by Jen Priester

For more information visit www.jenpriester.com

All rights reserved.

No portion of this book may be reproduced in any form without permission from Author.

For permission contact Jen@jenPphoto.com

Written, produced, and printed in the U.S.A.

To Holy Spirit, my Bestest Friend, who taught me who He is through the Word of God and what it means to believe His promises.
And for my dad, the best in the world!

God is happy and sings over me!
Zephaniah 3:17

You are always singing over me. I am so special to You, and You are always happy when we talk to each other. You are my best Friend!

He is a good Father and runs to give me a kiss!
Luke 15:20

You are the best Father! You are always on my side. When I come, You will always greet me with a hug and kiss. You love to be with me!

His door is always open and I can bravely come to Him anytime!
Hebrews 4:16

I love how I can always come to You when I'm sad, happy, and even scared. Your door is always open and You love to talk with me. You are always there for me!

God doesn't just love me, He likes me, too!
Isaiah 62:4

You don't just love me, You enjoy being with me! You like everything about me, and You made me just the way I am. I am special and unique to You!

God put me on earth so I would look for Him, reach out to Him, and find Him! He is never far from me!
Acts 17:26-27

When you made me, You had a purpose in mind. I'm not here by accident! You are never far from me, and You are so close I can reach out for You. You always want to be found by me!

I hear God's voice because I am His sheep.
John 10:27

I am Your sheep, and You are my Shepherd. I hear Your Voice and follow what You say. I love to be Yours! You will always come looking for me if I get stuck!

God even hears me when I talk to Him!
Psalm 34:17

I can talk to You anytime! You hear me, because I belong to You. If I am in trouble, I can call out to You and You hear me! You will always rescue me!

When I am with God, I am very happy!
Psalm 21:6

I was made to be Your friend. Being with You makes me happy, just as You being with me makes You happy! You love to have fun with me!

Nothing can ever take me from God's hands.
John 10:29

I never have to be scared because I'm safe with You. Nobody can ever take me from Your Strong Hands. Since You are always with me, I never have to fear anything!

God carries me on His shoulders!
Deuteronomy 33:12

I can rest in You because You shelter me. I am Your beloved. You carry me on Your Shoulders and I am secure!

He is always there to lift my head.
Psalm 3:3

No matter what happens, You will always be my greatest encouragement. When I am sad, You lift my head to show me Your goodness! You are my Shield!

God guides me by holding my hand.
Psalm 73:23-24

I am always with You! You hold me by my hand and guide me everywhere I go. We are so close and always together!

He even knows how many hairs I have on my head!
Matthew 10:30

You lovingly created me. You know everything about me! You even know how many hairs are on my head! My life was written by You in a book. Your plans for me are good!

God loved me so much He came to Earth and died for me!
John 3:16

You love me so much! You left Heaven to come to earth for me! You lived Your life among us, You died, and rose from the dead because it would win me back to You. I was the joy set before You!

And I will live with Him forever!
Revelation 21:3

I get to live with You forever in Heaven someday. But even now, You are always with me, and I don't have to wait until Heaven. I can know and hear You now! You are my Friend forever!

The End